TABLE OF CONTENT

Chapter 1: Introduction 8

Overview of Alvin Ailey's impact on African-American dance and social justice 8

Background on Ailey's life and career .. 10

Importance of his contributions to modern dance 12

Chapter 2: Early Life and Education 15

Ailey's childhood and early exposure to dance 15

Training and education in dance technique and choreography 18

Influence of his cultural background on his artistic expression 21

Chapter 3: The Birth of Alvin Ailey American Dance Theater 24

Formation of the dance company and its mission 24

Ailey's vision for celebrating African-American culture through dance...... 27

Early performances and reception by the public 30

Chapter 4: Choreographing Revelations 33

Evolution of Ailey's iconic masterpiece, "Revelations".............. 33

Exploration of the themes of spirituality, community, and resilience in the choreography 35

Impact of "Revelations" on audiences and the dance community............ 38

Chapter 5: Social Justice and Activism in Ailey's Work 41

Ailey's commitment to addressing social issues through dance............ 41

Representation of civil rights struggles and African-American heritage in his choreography......... 44

Collaboration with other artists and activists in promoting social justice.................. 46

Chapter 6: Legacy and Influence on the Dance Community 49

Ailey's lasting impact on modern dance and choreography.. 49

Continued relevance of his work in addressing contemporary social justice issues 52

Influence on future generations of dancers and choreographers 54

Chapter 7: The Pioneer of African-American Dance 58

Ailey's role in breaking barriers and creating opportunities for African-American dancers 58

Celebration of diversity and inclusivity in his dance company 61

Contributions to the cultural heritage of African-American performing arts 63

Chapter 8: The Alvin Ailey American Dance Theater Experience 66

Behind-the-scenes look at the company's rehearsals, performances, and tours 66

Training techniques and artistic vision of the company's artistic directors 70

Impact of the company's outreach and education programs on diverse communities 73

Chapter 9: Inspiration and Expression in Alvin Ailey's Choreography 78

Exploration of Ailey's unique choreographic style and movement techniques 78

Use of dance as a form of personal expression and storytelling 81

Influence of African and African-American dance traditions on his work 84

Chapter 10: Community Engagement and Cultural Exchange 88

Ailey's commitment to engaging with local communities through dance education and outreach 88

International tours and collaborations to promote cultural exchange and understanding 92

Influence of different cultural traditions on Ailey's choreography and artistic vision .. 95

Chapter 11: Theatrical Productions and Collaborations 100

Ailey's collaborations with other artists, musicians, and designers in creating theatrical productions 100

Exploration of diverse themes and styles in his choreography for the stage 104

Impact of staging and visual design on the overall experience of Ailey's performances 107

Chapter 12: Revisiting New York: Ailey's Homecoming 112

Ailey's connection to the cultural landscape of New York City 112

Relationship with other arts organizations and venues in New York 116

Impact of the city's diversity and energy on his artistic inspiration.................................... 120

Chapter 13: Maintaining Ailey's Vision: The Future of African-American Dance................ 124

Challenges and opportunities facing African-American dancers and choreographers today... 124

Importance of preserving Ailey's legacy and artistic vision for future generations. 129

Strategies for promoting diversity, equity, and inclusion in the dance community 133

Conclusion... 137

Reflecting on the enduring significance of Alvin Ailey's contributions to African-American dance and social justice...................................... 137

Call to action for continuing his mission of cultural exchange, education, and artistic excellence 141

Acknowledgment of Ailey's lasting impact on the world of dance and his legacy as a pioneer and visionary 143

Chapter 1: Introduction

Overview of Alvin Ailey's impact on African-American dance and social justice

Alvin Ailey's profound impact on African-American dance and social justice reverberates through the annals of dance history. His pioneering choreography, particularly the iconic "Revelations," not only celebrated the rich cultural heritage of the African diaspora but also became a poignant testament to the struggles and resilience of the Black community.

Ailey's unique movement vocabulary, rooted in African and Caribbean traditions, infused modern dance with an expressive authenticity that captivated audiences worldwide. His choreography transcended mere entertainment, becoming a powerful tool for social commentary and activism. "Revelations," a masterpiece of dance theater, wove together spirituals, gospel music, and evocative imagery to depict the complexities of the Black experience in America.

Beyond his groundbreaking artistry, Ailey dedicated his life to fostering social justice through the arts. He established the Alvin Ailey American Dance Theater, a multiracial company that provided a platform for talented Black dancers and choreographers. Through extensive touring and educational outreach programs, the company became a beacon of artistic excellence and cultural diversity, challenging racial stereotypes and inspiring generations of young people.

Ailey's legacy extends far beyond his lifetime. His pioneering work continues to inspire countless artists and activists, who recognize the transformative power of dance as a catalyst for social change. His unwavering commitment to cultural preservation and social justice ensures that his impact will continue to resonate for generations to come.

Background on Ailey's life and career

Alvin Ailey, born on January 5, 1931, in Rogers, Texas, was an extraordinary dancer, choreographer, and artistic director who left an indelible mark on the world of dance and social justice. His life's journey, marked by both triumph and adversity, shaped his artistic vision and fueled his unwavering commitment to using dance as a powerful tool for cultural expression, community building, and social change.

Growing up in the segregated South during the Jim Crow era, Ailey faced countless challenges and prejudices. Despite these obstacles, he discovered his passion for dance at an early age, finding solace and liberation in its transformative power. Inspired by the legendary Katherine Dunham, Ailey left Texas for Los Angeles in 1953, where he immersed himself in the vibrant dance scene, studying under renowned choreographers such as Lester Horton and Bella Lewitzky.

Ailey's unique style, characterized by its emotional depth, athleticism, and raw energy, quickly garnered attention. In 1958, he founded the Alvin Ailey American Dance Theater (AAADT), a groundbreaking company that showcased the talents of African American dancers and celebrated the diverse cultural heritage of the United States. With AAADT, Ailey created iconic works such as "Revelations," a powerful tribute to the African American experience, and "Cry," a poignant exploration of racial injustice.

Beyond his artistic achievements, Ailey was a passionate advocate for social justice. He believed that dance had the power to transcend racial and cultural barriers, fostering empathy and understanding. Through the AAADT, he provided a platform for African American dancers to share their stories and experiences, challenging prevailing stereotypes and promoting equality. Ailey also established the Ailey School, a renowned dance education center that has nurtured generations of dancers, ensuring the legacy of his artistic vision.

Ailey's life and work continue to inspire and resonate with audiences worldwide. His innovative choreography, groundbreaking company, and unwavering commitment to social justice have solidified his place as a true pioneer in the world of dance and a symbol of the transformative power of art.

Importance of his contributions to modern dance

Alvin Ailey's contributions to modern dance are immense and multifaceted, revolutionizing the art form and leaving an indelible mark on the cultural landscape. His groundbreaking choreography, particularly "Revelations," not only showcased the beauty and power of African

American dance but also became a testament to the resilience and struggles of his community. Through his innovative technique and exploration of social justice themes, Ailey challenged societal norms, fostered inclusivity, and paved the way for future generations of dancers and artists.

Ailey's unique choreographic style blended elements of African, Caribbean, and modern dance, creating a vibrant and expressive vocabulary that captured the essence of the African American experience. His signature work, "Revelations," is a masterpiece that pays homage to the Southern Black Church and its spiritual traditions. The piece's evocative movements, soulful music, and deeply personal narrative resonated with audiences worldwide, transcending cultural and racial boundaries.

Beyond his groundbreaking choreography, Ailey's dedication to education and community outreach played a pivotal role in his legacy. He founded the Alvin Ailey American Dance Theater, a multiracial company that provided opportunities for talented dancers of all backgrounds. Through extensive touring and educational programs, Ailey's company brought the beauty and power of dance to underserved communities, inspiring countless young people and fostering a love for the arts.

Ailey's commitment to social justice infused his work, using dance as a platform to address issues of race, equality, and human rights. His choreography often explored themes of discrimination, prejudice, and the search for identity, challenging audiences to confront uncomfortable truths and promoting understanding and empathy. By giving voice to the marginalized through his art, Ailey became an advocate for social change and a beacon of hope for those seeking justice.

Ailey's influence extended beyond the stage, as he became a cultural icon and a source of inspiration for generations of artists and activists. His innovative choreography, commitment to diversity, and dedication to social justice continue to shape the landscape of modern dance and inspire countless individuals to pursue their passions, embrace their identities, and strive for a more just and equitable world.

Chapter 2: Early Life and Education

Ailey's childhood and early exposure to dance

In the heart of rural Texas, amidst the rolling hills and cotton fields, Alvin Ailey's childhood was marked by the rhythms of a life deeply intertwined with the land and the vibrant cultural tapestry of his African American heritage. Born on January 5, 1931, in Rogers, a small town on the outskirts of Waco, Ailey spent his formative years surrounded by the warmth and love of his extended family. His mother, Lula Elizabeth Ailey, was a devout Christian woman who instilled in her son a strong sense of faith and community. Despite the challenges faced by

African Americans during that era, Lula's unwavering determination and resilience provided a solid foundation for her young son.

From a tender age, Ailey exhibited an innate affinity for movement and music. The melodies of gospel hymns and the rhythmic cadences of work songs that filled the air during church services and family gatherings ignited a spark within him. He would often lose himself in the expressive gestures and intricate footwork of the churchgoers, their bodies swaying and stomping in unison, embodying the spirit of their 信仰。It was through these early experiences that Ailey's passion for dance began to take shape.

As Ailey grew older, his fascination with dance only intensified. He would sneak out of the house to attend local dance parties, where he would marvel at the fluidity and grace of the older dancers. Their uninhibited movements and the way they seemed to effortlessly glide across the floor captivated his imagination. Ailey's enthusiasm for dance was further fueled by his exposure to Hollywood musicals, which showcased the glamour and spectacle of professional dance. The iconic performances of Fred Astaire and Gene Kelly left an indelible mark on his young mind, inspiring him to dream of one day becoming a dancer himself.

Ailey's formal dance training began in Los Angeles, where he moved with his mother at the age of 12. There, he enrolled in the Lester Horton Dance Theater, a renowned studio that fostered a vibrant and innovative approach to modern dance. Horton's unique technique, which emphasized the use of isolations, polycentrism, and improvisation, proved to be a perfect fit for Ailey's natural abilities. Under Horton's tutelage, Ailey's technical skills and artistic expression blossomed, laying the groundwork for his future choreographic endeavors.

Ailey's early exposure to dance, both within his family and community and through his formal training, laid the foundation for his remarkable career as a dancer and choreographer. The rhythms, movements, and stories that shaped his childhood experiences became the wellspring of inspiration for his groundbreaking works, which celebrated the beauty, strength, and resilience of the African

American experience. Through his iconic masterpiece, "Revelations," Ailey paid homage to his cultural heritage, creating a timeless work of art that continues to inspire and move audiences worldwide.

Training and education in dance technique and choreography

Alvin Ailey's early experiences with dance were transformative, shaping his future path as a dancer, choreographer, and artistic visionary. Growing up in Rogers, Texas, he was exposed to various forms of dance, including folk, spiritual, and social dances. These early encounters instilled in him a deep appreciation for the expressive power of movement.

His formal dance training began in 1949 when he enrolled at the Lester Horton Dance Theater in Los Angeles. Horton's innovative approach to dance, which emphasized freedom of expression and improvisation, proved to be a profound influence on Ailey. He embraced

Horton's focus on body awareness, kinesthetic intelligence, and the exploration of movement as a means of emotional expression.

Under Horton's guidance, Ailey developed a solid foundation in modern dance technique, which became the cornerstone of his choreographic style. He studied Horton's unique vocabulary of movements, characterized by its fluidity, dynamism, and percussive qualities. This training laid the groundwork for Ailey's signature style, which blended elements of African American vernacular dance with modern dance technique, creating a distinct and expressive movement language.

Ailey's insatiable curiosity led him to seek further training opportunities. He enrolled at the Hanya Holm Studio, where he studied Holm's technique, renowned for its clarity, precision, and emphasis on spatial relationships. Holm's teachings complemented his earlier training, refining his sense of balance, coordination, and spatial awareness.

His exposure to diverse dance styles extended beyond modern dance. He took classes in ballet, jazz, and Afro-Cuban dance, expanding his movement vocabulary and broadening his understanding of different dance traditions. This eclectic training allowed him to draw inspiration from multiple sources, enriching his choreographic vision.

In 1958, Ailey received a scholarship to attend the Martha Graham School of Contemporary Dance. Graham's technique, with its focus on contraction and release, proved to be another transformative influence on Ailey's development as a dancer. He admired Graham's ability to convey complex emotions and narratives through movement, an aspect that would become central to his own choreographic work.

Ailey's rigorous training and education in dance technique and choreography provided him with a comprehensive foundation upon which he built his extraordinary career. His deep understanding of movement, combined with his artistic vision and commitment to social justice, enabled him to create powerful and evocative works that continue to inspire and resonate with audiences worldwide.

Influence of his cultural background on his artistic expression

Alvin Ailey's cultural background as an African American man profoundly influenced his artistic expression as a dancer and choreographer. His early life experiences in rural Texas and his exposure to the rich traditions of African American music, dance, and storytelling shaped his unique artistic vision. Ailey's work celebrated the beauty, resilience, and struggles of the African American community, and he used his art as a platform to advocate for social justice.

Ailey's choreography often drew inspiration from the rhythms, movements, and spirituals of the African American church. His signature work, "Revelations," is a powerful testament to the enduring strength and faith of the African American people. The piece incorporates elements of traditional African dance, gospel music, and spoken word, creating a deeply moving and emotionally resonant experience.

Ailey's work also reflected his experiences of racism and discrimination. He often used his choreography to challenge stereotypes and to give voice to the voiceless. His piece "Cry" is a powerful indictment of police brutality and racial violence, while "Memoria" explores the legacy of slavery and the ongoing struggle for equality.

Through his work, Ailey not only celebrated African American culture but also used his art to promote understanding, compassion, and social change. He believed that dance had the power to break down barriers and to create a more just and equitable society. Ailey's legacy as a pioneer of modern dance and a tireless advocate for social justice continues to inspire artists and activists alike.

In addition to his work as a choreographer, Ailey was also a dedicated educator. He founded the Alvin Ailey American Dance Theater in 1958, which has become one of the most prestigious dance companies in the world. Ailey believed that dance was an essential part of a well-rounded education, and he worked tirelessly to make dance accessible to all.

The Alvin Ailey American Dance Theater has toured extensively throughout the United States and abroad, bringing Ailey's work to a global audience. The company has also been instrumental in training and mentoring young dancers, many of whom have gone on to become successful choreographers and performers in their own right.

Alvin Ailey's influence on the world of dance is immeasurable. He was a pioneer of modern dance, a tireless advocate for social justice, and a dedicated educator. His work continues to inspire and move audiences around the world, and his legacy as a dancer, choreographer, and social activist will continue to be celebrated for generations to come.

Chapter 3: The Birth of Alvin Ailey American Dance Theater

Formation of the dance company and its mission

In the annals of American dance, the formation of the Alvin Ailey American Dance Theater stands as a transformative moment, a testament to the indomitable spirit of its founder and the profound impact of African American dance on the global cultural landscape.

Alvin Ailey's vision for a company that celebrated the unique cultural heritage and artistic expression of African Americans emerged from his own experiences as a dancer and choreographer. Having trained under the tutelage of legendary modern dance pioneers such as Martha Graham and Lester Horton, Ailey sought to create a space where dancers of color could showcase their artistry and share their stories with the world.

In 1958, Ailey assembled a group of talented young dancers in New York City, forming the Alvin Ailey American Dance Theater. The company's mission was clear: to preserve and celebrate the African American dance tradition while also pushing the boundaries of modern dance and challenging societal norms.

Central to Ailey's artistic vision was the belief that dance was a powerful tool for social justice and cultural understanding. Through the company's performances, Ailey aimed to break down barriers of race and prejudice, fostering empathy and inspiring audiences to embrace diversity.

One of the company's most iconic works, "Revelations," encapsulates Ailey's commitment to both artistic excellence and social justice.

Premiering in 1960, "Revelations" is a celebration of the African American spiritual experience, blending elements of traditional African dance, gospel music, and modern dance. Through its evocative choreography and deeply emotional performances, "Revelations" has become a symbol of resilience, faith, and the enduring power of the human spirit.

Beyond its stage performances, the Alvin Ailey American Dance Theater has also played a pivotal role in dance education and community outreach. The company's educational programs provide opportunities for young dancers to learn about and experience the African American dance tradition, fostering a new generation of artists and cultural ambassadors.

The company's commitment to community engagement extends to its performances and collaborations with local organizations. Through these initiatives, the Alvin Ailey American Dance Theater brings the transformative power of dance to underserved communities, fostering a sense of belonging and inspiring social change.

Over the decades, the Alvin Ailey American Dance Theater has become a global cultural institution, performing to sold-out audiences around the world. The company's legacy as a pioneer of African American dance and a champion of social justice continues to inspire countless artists and audiences alike. Alvin Ailey's vision has not only transformed the dance world but has also left an enduring mark on the cultural fabric of America and beyond.

Ailey's vision for celebrating African-American culture through dance

Alvin Ailey's groundbreaking vision for dance extended far beyond the stage; he envisioned it as a potent force for celebrating, preserving, and uplifting African-American culture. His unwavering belief in the power of dance as a vehicle for social justice propelled him to create a company that would not only showcase the extraordinary talent and artistry of Black dancers but also serve as a testament to the resilience and creativity of the African-American experience.

Ailey's vision for his company was deeply rooted in his own experiences as a young African-American artist coming of age in the mid-twentieth century. He witnessed firsthand the pervasive racism and discrimination that limited opportunities for Black performers and stifled their creative expression. Determined to challenge these barriers, Ailey sought to create a platform where Black dancers could freely explore their artistry and share their unique cultural heritage with the world.

Central to Ailey's vision was the notion of authenticity. He believed that African-American dance should not merely imitate European forms but should draw upon the rich movement traditions and cultural practices of the African diaspora. Ailey's signature work, "Revelations," exemplifies this commitment to authenticity, paying homage to the spirituals, blues, and folk dances that shaped the African-American experience. Through its evocative choreography and soulful music, "Revelations" became a powerful testament to the resilience and expressiveness of Black culture.

Ailey's vision for his company also encompassed a deep commitment to education and community outreach. He recognized that dance could be a transformative force in the lives of young people, particularly those from underprivileged backgrounds. Through the Ailey School and the Ailey Extension program, he provided scholarships and accessible dance classes to aspiring dancers from all walks of life. Ailey believed that by nurturing the next generation of dancers, he was not only preserving the legacy of African-American dance but also empowering future generations to use their artistry as a force for positive change.

Ailey's unwavering dedication to his vision has left an enduring legacy in the world of dance and beyond. The Alvin Ailey American Dance Theater continues to tour globally, captivating audiences with its virtuosic performances and powerful storytelling. The company has become a symbol of excellence in African-American dance and a beacon of hope and inspiration for aspiring dancers of all backgrounds. Ailey's vision for a dance company that celebrates African-American culture and empowers its community has been realized, and his legacy continues to inspire and uplift generations of artists and audiences alike.

Early performances and reception by the public

Alvin Ailey's early performances electrified audiences, igniting a passion for modern dance and leaving an enduring legacy on the American cultural landscape. The premiere of "Revelations" in 1960 marked a watershed moment, captivating audiences with its powerful fusion of African-American spirituals, blues, and modern dance techniques. Ailey's choreography showcased the beauty, strength, and resilience of the African-American experience, resonating deeply with audiences across racial and cultural divides.

The public's enthusiastic reception to "Revelations" and subsequent Ailey performances propelled the company to national and international acclaim. Ailey's groundbreaking choreography challenged conventional notions of dance, merging elements of ballet, jazz, and African dance to create a unique and expressive style. His works celebrated the rich cultural heritage of African Americans, while also exploring universal themes of love, loss, and triumph.

Critics lauded Ailey's innovative approach and the technical virtuosity of his dancers. Anna Kisselgoff of The New York Times praised "Revelations" as "a stunning achievement. a masterpiece of American dance," while Clive Barnes of the New York Post hailed Ailey's choreography as "a revelation. a work of art that is both beautiful and moving. ".

Audiences were captivated by the raw emotion and authenticity conveyed through Ailey's dances. His company's performances became a catalyst for social change, fostering greater understanding and empathy between different cultures. Ailey's commitment to education and outreach programs ensured that his legacy extended beyond the stage, inspiring countless young people to pursue careers in dance.

The early performances of Alvin Ailey American Dance Theater were a testament to the transformative power of art. Ailey's choreography shattered boundaries, ignited social dialogue, and left an enduring mark on the world of dance. His legacy continues to inspire generations of artists and audiences, ensuring that his vision of a more just and equitable society through the power of movement remains alive.

Chapter 4: Choreographing Revelations

Evolution of Ailey's iconic masterpiece, "Revelations"

Alvin Ailey's "Revelations" has undergone a profound evolution since its inception in 1960, reflecting the choreographer's artistic journey, the changing social landscape, and the evolving perspectives on African American identity and culture.

Initially inspired by Ailey's childhood memories of Southern Black church services, "Revelations" initially showcased the spirituals, shouts, and gospel music that permeated these sacred spaces. Through the incorporation of traditional African American dance forms such as the cakewalk and ring shout, Ailey infused the work with a deep sense of cultural authenticity.

As Ailey's career progressed and his company gained international recognition, "Revelations" evolved to encompass a broader range of themes and influences. The 1972 revival of the work featured new sections that explored the struggles and triumphs of the Civil Rights Movement, highlighting the resilience and determination of the African American community. Ailey's choreography became more sophisticated, incorporating elements of modern dance and ballet, while retaining the emotional and spiritual core of the original piece.

Throughout its evolution, "Revelations" has remained a testament to Ailey's commitment to social justice and community engagement. The work has been performed in countless schools, churches, and community centers, reaching audiences that might not otherwise have access to the world of dance. Through its powerful storytelling and evocative movement, "Revelations" has fostered a greater understanding of African American history and culture, challenging stereotypes and promoting a message of unity and hope.

As the Alvin Ailey American Dance Theater continues to perform "Revelations," the work continues to resonate with audiences worldwide. It stands as a testament to Ailey's choreographic genius and his unwavering belief in the transformative power of dance. Through its enduring legacy, "Revelations" serves as a poignant reminder of the enduring struggle for social justice and the resilience of the human spirit.

Exploration of the themes of spirituality, community, and resilience in the choreography

Alvin Ailey's masterpiece, Revelations, transcends the realm of mere dance, embodying a profound exploration of spirituality, community, and resilience. This seminal work captures the essence of the African-American experience, intertwining movement, music, and cultural heritage to evoke a multidimensional narrative that resonates with audiences on a deeply personal level.

Spirituality: A Transcendent Expression.

Revelations exudes a palpable sense of spirituality, drawing inspiration from the rich traditions of the Southern Black Church. The choreography seamlessly incorporates elements of worship, from the rhythmic stomps and claps that evoke the fervor of spirituals to the sweeping arm gestures that mimic the fervor of prayer. Each dancer becomes a conduit for expressing the collective yearning for transcendence, conveying a profound connection to a higher power through their emotive movements.

Community: A Bond Unbreakable.

Ailey's choreography celebrates the indomitable spirit of community, showcasing the power of unity in the face of adversity. The dancers move in unison, their bodies forming a cohesive whole, symbolizing the resilience and interdependence that sustains African-American communities. Through intricate group formations and communal gestures, Revelations conveys a sense of shared history, struggle, and triumph, forging an unbreakable bond between the performers and the audience.

Resilience: An Unyielding Spirit.

Revelations is a testament to the resilience of the African-American spirit, honoring the ability to rise above adversity and emerge stronger. The choreography embodies the struggles and triumphs of the Black experience, from the pain of slavery to the hope of liberation. The dancers' powerful movements convey a defiance against oppression, a refusal to be broken, and an unwavering determination to persevere. Each step, each turn, and each leap becomes a symbol of resilience, reminding us of the indomitable spirit that has sustained African-Americans throughout history.

Through its evocative choreography, the piece transcends the realm of dance, becoming a powerful expression of the African-American experience. Revelations not only celebrates the beauty and strength of this vibrant culture but also serves as a reminder of the transformative power of art to inspire, unite, and empower.

Impact of "Revelations" on audiences and the dance community

Alvin Ailey's groundbreaking masterpiece, "Revelations," has left an indelible mark on the hearts and minds of audiences and the dance community alike. Since its premiere in 1960, this seminal work has captivated generations with its profound emotional resonance, masterful choreography, and unwavering commitment to social justice.

"Revelations" has profoundly impacted audiences through its evocative portrayal of the African American experience. Ailey's deeply personal choreography draws upon the rich traditions of African American culture, from spirituals to gospel to blues. The work's iconic movements, such as the "Wade in the Water" and the "Sinner Man," have become synonymous with the struggle for equality and the resilience of the human spirit. Audiences are left deeply moved by the work's raw emotion and its ability to bridge cultural divides.

Within the dance community, "Revelations" has been a transformative force. Ailey's innovative choreography has expanded the boundaries of modern dance, challenging traditional notions of form and technique. The work's emphasis on African American movement vocabulary has inspired countless choreographers to explore their own cultural heritage and to create works that celebrate diversity.

"Revelations" has also played a vital role in educating audiences about the history and culture of African Americans. Through its performances and educational programs, the Alvin Ailey American Dance Theater has brought this important work to communities across the world, fostering a greater understanding of the African American experience.

The impact of "Revelations" extends beyond the stage. The work has become a symbol of hope and inspiration for people of all backgrounds. Its message of unity, resilience, and the power of art to transform society has resonated with audiences worldwide.

Alvin Ailey's "Revelations" stands as a testament to the transformative power of dance. Its profound impact on audiences and the dance community has solidified its place as a masterpiece that continues to inspire, educate, and ignite social change.

Chapter 5: Social Justice and Activism in Ailey's Work

Ailey's commitment to addressing social issues through dance

Alvin Ailey's profound commitment to addressing social issues through the medium of dance is a testament to his artistry and unwavering belief in the transformative power of art. Ailey's work transcended mere entertainment, becoming a potent force for social justice, cultural preservation, and the empowerment of marginalized communities.

One of Ailey's most renowned choreographies, "Revelations," stands as a testament to his deep connection to the African American experience. The piece is a stirring tribute to the struggles, joys, and spiritual traditions of the African diaspora. Through its evocative movements and haunting music, "Revelations" sheds light on the resilience and indomitable spirit of a people grappling with the legacy of slavery and oppression. Ailey's genius lay in his ability to translate the complexities of the African American experience into a universal language of movement, making "Revelations" a poignant exploration of shared human experiences.

Ailey's commitment to social justice extended beyond the stage. He recognized the transformative potential of dance as a tool for education and community empowerment. In 1969, he founded the Alvin Ailey American Dance Theater, a groundbreaking company that provided a platform for African American dancers and choreographers. The company's mission was not only to showcase the beauty and athleticism of African American dance but also to use dance as a means of social commentary and activism. Through its performances, workshops, and educational programs, the Alvin Ailey American Dance Theater has played a pivotal role in fostering a greater understanding and appreciation of African American culture.

Ailey's unwavering commitment to social justice also manifested in his support for the civil rights movement. He actively participated in marches and rallies, and his work often reflected the struggles for equality and justice. Ailey believed that art could not be divorced from the social and political realities of its time, and he used his platform to amplify the voices of the marginalized and advocate for change.

Ailey's legacy as a pioneer of social justice through dance continues to inspire and empower artists and activists worldwide. His work serves as a reminder of the profound impact that art can have on society, challenging us to confront social issues, foster inclusivity, and strive for a more just and equitable world. Alvin Ailey's commitment to addressing social issues through dance stands as a testament to his artistry, activism, and unwavering belief in the transformative power of human expression.

Representation of civil rights struggles and African-American heritage in his choreography

Alvin Ailey's choreography powerfully reflects the complexities of African-American experiences, embodying the struggles for civil rights and celebrating the richness of their cultural heritage. His seminal work, "Revelations," stands as a poignant testament to the resilience and spirituality of the African-American community.

Through evocative movements, Ailey captures the essence of Southern Black Church rituals, gospel music, and the hardships faced by African Americans. The piece interweaves moments of joyous celebration with expressions of pain and sorrow, mirroring the multifaceted nature of the African-American experience.

Beyond "Revelations," Ailey's choreography consistently explored themes of social justice and equality. "Cry," for instance, confronts police brutality and racial injustice, while "Memoria" pays homage to those lost to the AIDS epidemic. Ailey's dances not only provided artistic expression but also served as a platform for activism, raising awareness and sparking dialogue on critical social issues.

Ailey's choreography also celebrated the strength and beauty of African-American culture. Works like "Suite Otis" and "The River" drew inspiration from African-American music, dance, and folklore, showcasing the richness and diversity of the African-American heritage. Ailey believed that dance could bridge cultural divides and promote understanding.

Through his innovative choreography and unwavering commitment to social justice, Alvin Ailey created a powerful legacy that continues to inspire and resonate with audiences today. His works not only represent the struggles and triumphs of African Americans but also serve as a testament to the transformative power of art in addressing societal issues and fostering cultural understanding.

Collaboration with other artists and activists in promoting social justice

Alvin Ailey's collaborations with other artists and activists played a pivotal role in promoting social justice through dance. His work with musicians, poets, visual artists, and community organizers amplified the impact of his choreography, extending its reach beyond the stage and into the broader cultural and political landscape.

One of Ailey's most significant collaborations was with the renowned jazz musician Duke Ellington. Together, they created "The River," a ballet that celebrated the history and resilience of the African American community. Ellington's evocative score provided a powerful backdrop for Ailey's choreography, which depicted the struggles and triumphs of Black Americans throughout history. The ballet's premiere in 1970 was a watershed moment, showcasing the transformative power of collaboration between dance and music in addressing social issues.

Ailey also collaborated with poets such as Maya Angelou and James Baldwin. Their words became an integral part of his performances, providing a literary dimension that deepened the emotional impact of his choreography. Angelou's poem "Caged Bird" inspired Ailey's solo "Cry," a poignant expression of the longing for freedom and self-expression. Baldwin's writings on race and identity informed Ailey's work, contributing to its incisive commentary on the social and political realities of Black America.

Ailey's collaborations extended beyond the arts world. He partnered with community activists and organizations to bring dance to underserved communities and promote social change. Through the Alvin Ailey American Dance Theater's educational outreach programs, he introduced dance to young people from diverse backgrounds, fostering their creativity and empowering them as agents of social justice.

Ailey's collaboration with the civil rights activist Martin Luther King Jr. was particularly impactful. King recognized the power of dance as a tool for social transformation and invited Ailey to perform at several events during the civil rights movement. Ailey's choreography became a powerful symbol of the movement's goals of equality and justice, inspiring audiences and galvanizing support for the cause.

Collaboration was central to Ailey's artistic and social justice mission. By working with other artists and activists, he created a multifaceted body of work that resonated deeply with audiences and challenged societal norms. His legacy as a pioneer of modern dance is inextricably linked to his commitment to using his art as a catalyst for social change.

Chapter 6: Legacy and Influence on the Dance Community

Ailey's lasting impact on modern dance and choreography

Alvin Ailey's profound impact on modern dance and choreography continues to reverberate through the contemporary landscape, leaving an indelible legacy that has shaped the very essence of the art form. His groundbreaking contributions have not only revolutionized the technical and aesthetic vocabulary of dance but have also propelled the visibility and recognition of African American artistry on global stages.

Ailey's choreographic genius manifested in his ability to fuse diverse movement traditions, seamlessly blending African, Caribbean, and modern dance techniques into a cohesive and expressive language. His signature work, "Revelations," stands as a testament to his mastery, paying homage to the rich spiritual and cultural heritage of the African American experience. Through its evocative storytelling and emotionally charged sequences, "Revelations" has become an iconic masterpiece that transcends time and continues to inspire generations of dancers and audiences alike.

Beyond his artistic innovations, Ailey's legacy extends to his unwavering commitment to social justice and community empowerment. He recognized the transformative power of dance as a vehicle for social change, establishing the Alvin Ailey American Dance Theater as a platform for artists of color to showcase their talents and challenge prevailing stereotypes. The company's mission to promote diversity and inclusion has had a profound impact on the dance world, fostering a sense of belonging and empowering marginalized voices.

Ailey's influence extends far beyond the confines of the stage. His educational initiatives, such as the Ailey School and the AileyCamp, have nurtured aspiring dancers and provided opportunities for underprivileged youth to engage with the art form. These programs have not only produced exceptional performers but have also cultivated a deep appreciation for dance within diverse communities.

The Alvin Ailey American Dance Theater continues to serve as a beacon of excellence, touring extensively and captivating audiences worldwide. The company's unwavering commitment to preserving Ailey's legacy while embracing contemporary voices has ensured that his artistic vision remains vibrant and relevant. Ailey's influence is evident in the works of countless choreographers who have drawn inspiration from his pioneering spirit, carrying forward his legacy of innovation and cultural expression.

His groundbreaking techniques, evocative storytelling, and unwavering commitment to social justice have left an indelible mark on the art form. His legacy continues to inspire generations of dancers, educators, and audiences, fostering a more inclusive and expressive dance landscape that celebrates the richness and diversity of the human experience.

Continued relevance of his work in addressing contemporary social justice issues

Alvin Ailey's choreographic masterpiece, "Revelations," continues to resonate deeply with contemporary audiences, offering a poignant exploration of the African American experience and its enduring relevance to broader social justice issues. Ailey's work transcends the boundaries of dance, delving into the realm of social commentary, cultural preservation, and the pursuit of racial equality.

Through its evocative movements and spiritual overtones, "Revelations" captures the essence of the African American journey, from the struggles of slavery to the triumphs of the Civil Rights Movement. Ailey's choreography masterfully intertwines elements of traditional African dance, jazz, and modern dance, creating a unique and powerful expression of cultural identity and resilience.

The work's continued relevance stems from its ability to address contemporary issues of racial injustice and social inequality. Its depiction of the challenges faced by African Americans resonates with audiences today, as the fight for racial justice remains a pressing concern. "Revelations" serves as a reminder of the ongoing struggle for equality and the need for continued activism.

Moreover, Ailey's emphasis on community and education through dance has left a lasting legacy in the dance world. The Alvin Ailey American Dance Theater, which he founded in 1958, continues to provide opportunities for dancers of all backgrounds to train, perform, and connect with audiences. The company's outreach programs bring dance education to underserved communities, fostering a sense of empowerment and artistic expression.

Ailey's work continues to inspire new generations of dancers and choreographers, who draw inspiration from his innovative approach and commitment to social justice. His legacy as a pioneer in modern dance and an advocate for equality ensures that his work will continue to resonate with audiences for years to come. "Revelations" remains a powerful testament to the transformative power of dance, its ability to illuminate social issues, and its enduring relevance in the pursuit of a more just and equitable society.

Influence on future generations of dancers and choreographers

Alvin Ailey's indelible mark on the dance world extends far beyond his own groundbreaking performances and choreography. As a pioneer in the field of modern dance, Ailey's influence has had a profound impact on generations of dancers and choreographers, shaping their artistic vision, technical prowess, and commitment to social justice.

Through his signature work, "Revelations," Ailey not only showcased the beauty and power of African-American dance forms but also provided a platform for young dancers to express their own unique voices. The piece's themes of resilience, community, and the search for identity resonated deeply with dancers and audiences alike, inspiring them to explore their own cultural heritage and use dance as a medium for personal expression.

Ailey's emphasis on technical excellence and artistic integrity set a high standard for aspiring dancers. His rigorous training regimen and innovative choreographic style challenged dancers to push their physical and creative limits, encouraging them to strive for both precision and artistry. This unwavering pursuit of excellence became a hallmark of Ailey's dancers, who carried his legacy of technical virtuosity into their own work.

Beyond his artistic influence, Ailey was also a tireless advocate for social justice. He believed that dance had the power to break down barriers, promote understanding, and foster a sense of community. Through his performances, workshops, and educational programs, Ailey sought to make dance accessible to all, regardless of race, background, or financial circumstances.

His unwavering commitment to diversity and inclusion inspired countless dancers to use their art to address social issues and advocate for change. The Alvin Ailey American Dance Theater became a beacon of artistic excellence and social consciousness, serving as a model for other dance companies and organizations.

Ailey's legacy continues to inspire dancers and choreographers today. His groundbreaking choreography, technical virtuosity, and unwavering commitment to social justice serve as a constant reminder of the transformative power of dance. His work has fostered a generation of artists who are not only exceptional dancers but also agents of change, using their art to uplift, empower, and inspire others.

As the dance world continues to evolve, Alvin Ailey's influence remains a guiding force, shaping the artistic aspirations and social consciousness of generations to come. His legacy is not merely a tribute to a legendary dancer and choreographer but a testament to the enduring power of dance to connect, inspire, and transform both individuals and society as a whole.

Chapter 7: The Pioneer of African-American Dance

Ailey's role in breaking barriers and creating opportunities for African-American dancers

Alvin Ailey's profound impact on the world of dance extended far beyond his remarkable choreography and captivating performances. He dedicated his life to breaking down racial barriers and creating opportunities for African-American dancers, transforming the dance landscape and leaving an enduring legacy of social justice and cultural empowerment.

Ailey's unwavering commitment to shattering stereotypes and dismantling prejudices began in his early days as a dancer. In a time when African-Americans faced systemic exclusion from the predominantly white world of dance, Ailey refused to be marginalized. He honed his craft with determination, training under the tutelage of legendary figures such as Martha Graham and Lester Horton. His exceptional talent and artistry earned him recognition, but he recognized the need for a dedicated platform for African-American dancers.

Driven by a deep sense of purpose, Ailey founded the Alvin Ailey American Dance Theater in 1958. This groundbreaking company became a beacon of hope and a symbol of resistance against racial inequality. By showcasing the extraordinary talents of African-American dancers, Ailey challenged prevailing notions and opened doors for countless aspiring artists. The company's diverse repertoire, which included Ailey's own iconic works like "Revelations" and "Blues Suite," celebrated the richness and complexity of the African-American experience.

Ailey's influence extended beyond the stage. He established the Ailey School in 1969, providing a nurturing environment for young dancers to develop their skills and pursue their dreams. The school's innovative curriculum emphasized not only technical proficiency but also cultural awareness and community engagement. Through its outreach programs, the Ailey School brought the transformative power of dance to underserved communities, inspiring and empowering countless young people.

Ailey's vision extended beyond the United States. He believed in the universality of dance as a language that transcends cultural boundaries. The Alvin Ailey American Dance Theater toured extensively, captivating audiences worldwide and fostering cross-cultural understanding. Ailey's choreography drew inspiration from diverse cultural traditions, reflecting his deep appreciation for the interconnectedness of human experience.

Ailey's legacy is not confined to the dance world. His unwavering advocacy for social justice and his belief in the transformative power of art made him an influential voice in the broader cultural landscape. He spoke out against racial injustice, supported civil rights movements, and used his platform to promote understanding and empathy. Ailey's activism extended beyond words; he actively supported organizations working to combat poverty, discrimination, and inequality.

Alvin Ailey's pioneering spirit, his unwavering commitment to breaking barriers, and his dedication to creating opportunities for African-American dancers have left an indelible mark on the world. His legacy continues to inspire and empower countless artists and advocates, serving as a testament to the transformative power of dance and the indomitable spirit of those who dare to challenge the status quo.

Celebration of diversity and inclusivity in his dance company

Alvin Ailey, an artistic visionary, recognized the power of dance as a universal language that could transcend cultural, social, and racial boundaries. Throughout his illustrious career, he championed diversity and inclusivity, transforming his dance company into a vibrant tapestry of cultures and backgrounds. His unwavering belief in the inherent worth and talent of all individuals regardless of their race, gender, or origin became a defining characteristic of the Alvin Ailey American Dance Theater.

Ailey's commitment to diversity extended beyond the stage. He understood that true inclusivity required creating a supportive and welcoming environment for all members of his company. He fostered a sense of community where dancers felt valued, respected, and empowered to express their unique identities through movement. This inclusive approach not only enriched the artistic output of the company but also created a space where dancers could thrive and grow as individuals.

Moreover, Ailey believed that diversity was not merely a matter of representation but also a source of artistic inspiration. He drew upon the diverse backgrounds and experiences of his dancers to create works that celebrated the richness and complexity of the African-

American experience. From the vibrant rhythms of African dance to the soulful melodies of gospel music, Ailey's choreography paid homage to the cultural heritage of his dancers while simultaneously pushing the boundaries of modern dance.

Through his groundbreaking work, Ailey not only challenged prevailing notions of race and identity but also inspired generations of dancers and audiences alike. His unwavering commitment to diversity and inclusivity left an indelible mark on the dance world, creating a legacy that continues to shape the landscape of contemporary dance today.

Contributions to the cultural heritage of African-American performing arts

Alvin Ailey, an African-American modern dance choreographer, dancer, and director, played a pivotal role in shaping the cultural heritage of African-American performing arts.

Ailey's contributions to the dance world are vast and multifaceted, including the creation of groundbreaking choreographies, the establishment of a renowned dance company, and the fostering of social justice through dance.

Ailey's choreographies are a testament to his artistic genius and his deep understanding of the African-American experience. His most celebrated work, "Revelations," is a masterpiece that fuses spirituals, blues, and traditional African dance movements to create a powerful and evocative exploration of the African-American journey. Ailey's other notable works include "Cry," "Blues Suite," and "Masekela Langage," each of which showcases his unique blend of athleticism, emotional depth, and storytelling ability.

Beyond his choreographic brilliance, Ailey was also a visionary leader in the dance world. In 1958, he founded the Alvin Ailey American Dance Theater, a multiracial company that became a beacon of diversity and excellence in the performing arts. The company provided a platform for African-American dancers to showcase their artistry and helped to break down racial barriers in the dance world.

Ailey's commitment to social justice was deeply intertwined with his artistic endeavors. He believed that dance had the power to transcend racial divides and promote understanding and empathy. Through his performances and educational programs, Ailey sought to use dance as a tool for social change. He established the Alvin Ailey American Dance Center, which provided training and scholarships to young dancers from diverse backgrounds.

Ailey's legacy continues to inspire generations of dancers and audiences alike. His choreographies have become iconic symbols of African-American culture, and his company remains a thriving force in the dance world. Ailey's dedication to artistic excellence, diversity, and social justice has left an indelible mark on the cultural landscape of America and beyond.

Chapter 8: The Alvin Ailey American Dance Theater Experience

Behind-the-scenes look at the company's rehearsals, performances, and tours

Alvin Ailey American Dance Theater, founded by the legendary choreographer Alvin Ailey in 1958, has become an iconic institution in the world of modern dance. Its groundbreaking performances and social justice advocacy have left an indelible mark on the cultural landscape. This chapter provides an exclusive glimpse behind the scenes of the company's rehearsals, performances, and tours, revealing the artistry, dedication, and transformative power that drive the Ailey dancers.

Rehearsals: A Crucible of Creativity and Collaboration.

Rehearsals are the lifeblood of the Ailey company, where dancers meticulously hone their technique and bring choreographic visions to life. The process is a rigorous one, requiring both physical and mental stamina. Dancers spend countless hours in the studio, working tirelessly to perfect their movements, explore emotional depth, and connect with the stories they are embodying.

Collaboration is paramount in the Ailey rehearsal process. Dancers work closely with choreographers, artistic directors, and each other, sharing ideas, offering feedback, and pushing the boundaries of their artistry. The atmosphere is one of mutual respect and trust, fostering an environment where dancers feel empowered to take risks and grow both individually and collectively.

Performances: Captivating Audiences with Dynamic Movement.

Ailey performances are electrifying experiences that showcase the company's virtuosity, passion, and commitment to social justice. On stage, the dancers transform into characters, embodying the human condition with raw emotion and technical brilliance.

Signature works like "Revelations" and "Blues Suite" are testaments to the company's African-American heritage, exploring themes of spirituality, resilience, and the struggle for equality. Each performance is infused with a sense of purpose, connecting audiences with the rich cultural traditions and social issues that have shaped the Ailey experience.

Tours: Ambassadors of Dance and Cultural Exchange.

The Ailey company embarks on extensive tours both nationally and internationally, sharing its artistry with diverse audiences. These tours serve as a platform for cultural exchange, fostering understanding and appreciation for the power of dance.

Dancers become ambassadors for the company and for the African-American dance tradition, connecting with communities from all walks of life. Through workshops, master classes, and outreach programs, they inspire young dancers and promote the importance of arts education.

Legacy and Impact: A Lasting Impression on the World.

Alvin Ailey American Dance Theater's legacy is one of artistic excellence, cultural preservation, and social justice advocacy. The company has played a pivotal role in shaping the landscape of modern dance, breaking down racial barriers and creating a platform for African-American artists.

Its performances and educational initiatives have touched countless lives, inspiring generations of dancers and audiences alike. The Ailey dancers embody the spirit of their founder, carrying on his vision of using dance as a force for unity, empowerment, and social change.

Through rigorous rehearsals, captivating performances, and transformative tours, the company continues to honor its founder's legacy, enriching the cultural landscape and empowering communities worldwide.

Training techniques and artistic vision of the company's artistic directors

Artistic Directors' Training Techniques.

Throughout its history, the Alvin Ailey American Dance Theater has been guided by a succession of artistic directors, each of whom has left their own unique mark on the company's training techniques.

Alvin Ailey: Ailey's training emphasized a strong technical foundation rooted in classical ballet, jazz, and modern dance. He believed that dancers should be versatile and expressive, able to convey a wide range of emotions and experiences through their movement.

Judith Jamison: Jamison, who succeeded Ailey as artistic director in 1989, continued to uphold the company's commitment to technical excellence. However, she also introduced new training methods that focused on developing dancers' artistry and individuality. Under Jamison's leadership, the company's dancers became known for their expressive qualities and their ability to connect with audiences on a deep level.

Robert Battle: Battle, who became artistic director in 2011, has maintained the company's high standards of technical training while also expanding the repertoire to include works by contemporary choreographers. Battle's training methods emphasize the importance of collaboration and improvisation, allowing dancers to explore their own creativity and contribute to the development of new works.

Artistic Vision.

The artistic directors of the Alvin Ailey American Dance Theater have shared a common commitment to using dance as a means of cultural expression and social justice.

Alvin Ailey: Ailey's choreography was often inspired by the African-American experience, and he used dance to explore themes of identity, community, and resilience. His signature work, "Revelations," is a powerful tribute to the Southern Black Church and its role in the Civil Rights Movement.

Judith Jamison: Jamison continued Ailey's legacy of using dance to address social issues, creating works that explored topics such as racism, poverty, and AIDS. She also expanded the company's repertoire to include works by choreographers from around the world, reflecting her belief in the universality of the human experience.

Robert Battle: Battle has continued to uphold the company's commitment to social justice, while also broadening its artistic vision to include a wider range of perspectives and experiences. Under Battle's leadership, the company has commissioned new works that explore themes of gender, sexuality, and immigration.

The training techniques and artistic vision of the Alvin Ailey American Dance Theater's artistic directors have shaped the company's identity and legacy. Through their emphasis on technical excellence, expressive artistry, and social justice, these directors have ensured that the company remains a vital force in the world of dance.

Impact of the company's outreach and education programs on diverse communities

The Alvin Ailey American Dance Theater, a renowned cultural institution in the world of dance, has had a significant impact on diverse communities through its outreach and education programs. In this essay, we will examine the various ways in which the company's outreach and education programs have enriched and empowered diverse communities, particularly in New York City.

First and foremost, the Alvin Ailey American Dance Theater's outreach and education programs play a pivotal role in preserving and promoting African American culture and the art of dance. Through the exploration of African American themes and stories, the company allows diverse communities to connect with their roots and heritage. By engaging with diverse choreographers and dancers, these programs create a platform for cultural exchange and dialogue, fostering a sense of belonging and pride within these communities.

One of the key contributions of the outreach and education programs is their focus on providing access to dance education and training, regardless of one's socio-economic background. The Alvin Ailey American Dance Theater believes in empowering individuals through movement, technique, and artistic expression. By offering scholarships and community programs, the company ensures that talent and potential are not limited by financial constraints. This commitment to inclusivity not only creates opportunities for aspiring dancers but also encourages diversity in the field of dance, breaking down barriers that have historically hindered underrepresented communities from pursuing careers in the performing arts.

Moreover, the company's outreach and education programs extend beyond the realm of dance training. They also serve as a vehicle for social change and advocacy, aligning with the concept of social justice. By working with various community organizations and schools, the Alvin Ailey American Dance Theater integrates dance into broader educational frameworks, addressing issues such as equality, empathy, and resilience. Through their performances and workshops, the company engages diverse audiences, promoting an understanding of the power of movement and its ability to transcend cultural and societal boundaries.

The legacy of Alvin Ailey, the pioneer behind this extraordinary dance theater, is at the heart of the impact these programs have on diverse communities. Ailey's own journey and experiences as an African American dancer have shaped the core values of the company, emphasizing inclusivity, artistic excellence, and social transformation. By showcasing Ailey's groundbreaking work, the outreach and education programs serve as an inspiration for aspiring dancers, educators, and community leaders alike. They highlight the transformative power of dance as a vehicle for personal and collective liberation.

Finally, the Alvin Ailey American Dance Theater's outreach and education programs create a sense of community, both within the company and among its audience members. Diverse communities come together through shared experiences, embracing the power of movement to connect, heal, and inspire. The company's performances often reflect the lived experiences of the community, enabling individuals to see their own stories reflected on stage. This sense of representation and belonging fosters a deep bond between the Alvin Ailey American Dance Theater and the communities it serves, leaving an indelible mark on the cultural fabric of New York City.

By preserving and promoting African American culture, providing access to dance education, advocating for social justice, and fostering a sense of community, the company has empowered individuals, transcended societal boundaries, and inspired generations to pursue their artistic passions. Through their commitment to diversity and inclusion, the Alvin Ailey American Dance Theater continues to play a vital role in promoting cultural understanding and celebrating the beauty and power of dance in all its forms.

Chapter 9: Inspiration and Expression in Alvin Ailey's Choreography

Exploration of Ailey's unique choreographic style and movement techniques

This chapter sheds light on how Ailey's works have showcased his cultural heritage, his commitment to social justice, and his ability to inspire and express through dance.

Ailey's choreography can be classified as modern dance, a genre that emerged as a rebellion against the rigidity of classical ballet. Ailey incorporated elements of African

American culture into his works, infusing his movements with a sense of rhythm, syncopation, and improvisation. This fusion of African and Western dance forms created a distinct style that was hailed for its authenticity and innovation.

The centerpiece of Ailey's choreographic style is his iconic work, "Revelations." This masterpiece captures the African American experience using movement and music, as it takes the audience on a journey through the joys, pains, and resilience of the black community. Ailey's use of wide-ranging movements, from soft and flowing to bold and dramatic, captures the emotional depth and power of the subject matter.

Ailey's movement techniques are heavily influenced by his training in Horton technique, a modern dance technique founded by Lester Horton. This technique emphasizes the importance of a strong center, groundedness, and the articulation of every part of the body. Ailey's dances are characterized by his dancers' technical precision, athleticism, and expressive use of the entire body.

Ailey's choreography also reflects his lifelong commitment to social justice and the pursuit of equality. Through his works, he sought to challenge racial stereotypes and advocate for the rights and dignity of African Americans. His dances celebrated the beauty and strength of black culture, as well as offering a commentary on the injustices faced by marginalized communities.

Moreover, Ailey used education as a tool for social change, as he created an environment where aspiring dancers, regardless of their background, could learn and develop their skills. He founded the Alvin Ailey American Dance Theater, a renowned institution that became a powerful force for diversity and inclusion in the dance world.

Ailey's performances left a lasting impact on audiences around the world. His choreography, infused with the spirit and history of the African American community, resonated deeply with people of all backgrounds. His works have been performed in prestigious theaters and festivals globally, cementing his reputation as a pioneer of African American dance.

Alvin Ailey's legacy extends far beyond his choreographic style and movement techniques. His commitment to social justice, his emphasis on community, and his dedication to nurturing the next generation of dancers continue to inspire and shape the world of dance. His visionary approach to dance has forever changed the landscape of modern artistry.

Ailey's dances reflect his cultural heritage and commitment to social justice, as he used movement to inspire and express the African American experience. His legacy as a pioneer of African American dance and his transformative impact on the dance world continue to influence and captivate audiences globally.

Use of dance as a form of personal expression and storytelling

Alvin Ailey, a pioneer in the world of modern dance, utilized his choreography to convey powerful messages and to shed light on African American culture and social issues. Through his innovative techniques and captivating performances, Ailey was able to inspire and connect with audiences on a profound level.

Central to Ailey's choreography was the marriage of movement and storytelling. He believed that dance had the power to communicate emotions and narratives in a way that words often couldn't. Ailey's pieces often drew from his own personal experiences as an African American man, as well as from the broader struggles faced by African Americans in society. His choreography served as a platform for exploration, reflection, and advocacy.

One of Ailey's most renowned works, "Revelations," is a testament to his use of dance as a form of personal expression and storytelling. This iconic piece, set to spirituals and gospel music, traces the journey of African Americans from slavery to freedom. Through a series of powerful and emotionally charged movements, Ailey was able to convey the resilience, hope, and strength of the African American community. "Revelations" is a powerful example of how dance can be used to engage with themes of cultural identity, social justice, and historical legacy.

Ailey's choreography also reflected his commitment to social justice and education. He believed in the transformative power of dance as a means of creating dialogue and fostering empathy. Through his performances and workshops, Ailey sought to educate and inspire his audience, encouraging them to think critically about the issues faced by marginalized communities. His work consistently challenged societal norms and provided a platform for marginalized voices to be heard.

Ailey's legacy as a pioneer in African American dance continues to live on through the Alvin Ailey American Dance Theater. This renowned dance company, based in New York, carries forward his commitment to using dance as a form of personal expression and storytelling. The Theater's repertoire often includes pieces that engage with issues of social justice, cultural heritage, and personal identity. Through their performances, the company continues to inspire and provoke thought, keeping Ailey's creative vision alive.

Through his innovative techniques, he was able to communicate emotions, narratives, and social messages in a way that resonated with audiences. Ailey's work continues to inspire and challenge, demonstrating the profound impact that dance can have in promoting social justice, fostering cultural understanding, and preserving a legacy of African American art.

Influence of African and African-American dance traditions on his work

Alvin Ailey, a prominent figure in the world of modern dance, had a deep connection to African and African-American dance traditions. This essay explores the profound impact of African and African-American dance on Ailey's work, highlighting his use of movement, technique, and cultural expression, as well as the social justice implications and legacy of his artistry.

Ailey's choreography is profoundly influenced by African and African-American dance traditions. Throughout his career, he incorporated movements and techniques rooted in these traditions, creating a unique and distinctive style. African dance, characterized by a combination of earthy and rhythmic movements, served as a foundation for Ailey's work. In his choreography, he skillfully blended these movements with elements of modern dance to create a seamless fusion of styles that celebrated both African and African-American culture.

One of Ailey's most notable works, "Revelations," clearly exemplifies the use of African and African-American dance traditions. Inspired by his own upbringing in rural Texas and the church services he attended, this piece is deeply rooted in African-American culture. The movements in "Revelations" portray the collective experience of African-Americans, capturing the struggles and triumphs of their history.

Ailey's commitment to cultural expression is evident in his choreographic choices. He drew upon African and African-American dance traditions to tell stories, convey emotions, and connect with his audience on a profound level. Through his movements, he offered a glimpse into the rich cultural heritage of African and African-American communities. By embracing these traditions, Ailey sought to provide a space for the expression of collective memories and experiences.

Apart from the artistic expression, Ailey's work also encompassed social justice themes. As an artist, he used his choreography as a tool for raising awareness about social issues, particularly those affecting African-Americans. By incorporating elements of African and African-American dance traditions, Ailey created powerful narratives that not only entertained but also prompted conversations about inequality and racial injustice.

Education played a vital role in Ailey's work, as he sought to empower future generations of dancers. He believed in the importance of preserving and passing on African and African-American dance traditions. Ailey established the Alvin Ailey American Dance Theater, a professional dance company that continues to thrive as a pioneer of African-American dance. Through the company's performances and educational initiatives, Ailey's legacy lives on, inspiring countless dancers and audiences alike.

Ailey's connection to the African and African-American dance traditions is deeply rooted in his community in New York. He was dedicated to giving back to the communities that nurtured him and supported his artistic vision. The Alvin Ailey American Dance Theater became a beacon of hope and an integral part of the cultural fabric of New York City, offering performances and artistic opportunities to diverse audiences.

His works, particularly "Revelations," exemplified his use of movement, technique, and cultural expression to tell stories and connect with his audience. Moreover, he used his artistry as a means of advocating for social justice and empowering future generations of dancers. Ailey's legacy, seen through the Alvin Ailey American Dance Theater, continues to inspire and uplift communities in New York and beyond.

Chapter 10: Community Engagement and Cultural Exchange

Ailey's commitment to engaging with local communities through dance education and outreach

" Through his pioneering work as a choreographer and his establishment of the Alvin Ailey American Dance Theater, Ailey sought to address social and cultural issues within his community using the powerful medium of dance.

A key aspect of Ailey's commitment to community engagement was his belief in the transformative power of dance. Ailey understood that dance had the ability to bring people together, break down barriers, and foster a sense of unity and understanding. He believed that through the movement and technique of dance, individuals could find both physical and emotional liberation. For Ailey, dance was not simply a form of entertainment, but a means of expression, a language through which he could convey messages about identity, history, and social justice.

African American culture and history played a significant role in Ailey's choreographic works. Ailey drew inspiration from the African American experience, infusing his dances with elements of African and African American culture. He sought to celebrate and honor the rich heritage of his community through his performances. Ailey's choreographic masterpiece, "Revelations," exemplifies his commitment to exploring African American history and culture through dance. This piece, which has become a hallmark of the Alvin Ailey American Dance Theater, is a reflection on the resilience and strength of African Americans in the face of adversity.

Education was another integral component of Ailey's community engagement efforts. Ailey believed that dance should be accessible to all, regardless of background or socioeconomic status. He recognized the importance of providing opportunities for individuals to learn and engage with the art form. In addition to his professional company, Ailey established the Ailey School, a dance academy that offered rigorous training to aspiring dancers of all ages. Through the school, Ailey aimed to not only nurture emerging talent but also instill a love and appreciation for dance in the broader community.

Outreach initiatives were also a key focus of Ailey's community engagement endeavors. He believed in taking dance beyond the confines of the theater and into non-traditional spaces. Ailey and his company often performed in schools, community centers, and public parks, bringing the beauty and power of dance directly to the people. By doing so, Ailey hoped to break down the perceived barriers between dance and the everyday lives of individuals in the community. His performances served as a catalyst for conversations about social justice, identity, and the human experience.

Ailey's commitment to community engagement continues to be relevant today. His legacy as a pioneer in the world of modern dance and as a champion of African American cultural expression lives on. The Alvin Ailey American Dance Theater remains a vital force in the dance world, continuing to engage with audiences and communities around the world. Ailey's dedication to using dance as a tool for social change serves as an inspiration for future generations of dancers, educators, and activists.

Through his choreography, Ailey celebrated African American culture and history, using dance as a means of expression and storytelling. He believed in the importance of making dance accessible to all through education and outreach initiatives. Ailey's legacy as a pioneer and his profound impact on the dance world and communities around the world continue to inspire and uplift.

International tours and collaborations to promote cultural exchange and understanding

This essay explores how these endeavors have impacted the dance world, specifically focusing on Alvin Ailey and his groundbreaking contributions to modern dance as an African American choreographer.

Alvin Ailey's masterpiece, "Revelations," stands as a testament to his cultural legacy and the power of movement to transcend boundaries. When Ailey first presented this piece in 1960, it stunned audiences and transformed the perception of African American art. Rooted in the African American experience, "Revelations" encompasses themes of spirituality, resilience, and hope. Its universal appeal lies in the sheer honesty of the choreography, which conveys emotions that resonate with people from all walks of life.

International tours have played a pivotal role in sharing Ailey's masterwork with audiences worldwide. The Alvin Ailey American Dance Theater has embarked on numerous tours, presenting "Revelations" to diverse communities across the globe. These performances have allowed people from different cultures and backgrounds to witness the beauty and significance of African American dance.

Collaborations have further enhanced Ailey's impact as a pioneer of cultural exchange. Through these partnerships, the Alvin Ailey American Dance Theater has joined forces with dance companies, artists, and organizations from around the world. By combining their unique artistic voices, these collaborations ignite a rich tapestry of ideas and movements, fostering a deeper understanding of diverse cultures.

Education plays a crucial role in international tours and collaborations, as they open doors for dancers and audiences to explore different dance techniques and traditions. Dancers involved in these exchanges benefit from exposure to new movement vocabularies, training methods, and artistic philosophies. This cross-pollination of ideas elevates their craft and broadens their understanding of dance as a global language.

Moreover, international tours and collaborations serve as platforms for social justice advocacy. Alvin Ailey persistently used his art to shed light on racial inequalities, social injustice, and inequities faced by marginalized communities. By traveling the world and sharing his choreography, Ailey encouraged dialogue on these critical issues, spurring conversations that led to change.

The impact of these tours and collaborations extends far beyond the performances themselves. They create lasting connections between the Alvin Ailey American Dance Theater and the communities they engage with. Through workshops, masterclasses, and outreach programs, the company fosters meaningful interactions, empowering individuals with the tools to share their stories through dance.

New York City, the birthplace of Alvin Ailey American Dance Theater, remains a central hub for these international collaborations. The city's vibrant dance scene attracts artists from around the world, offering a melting pot of diverse experiences and perspectives. Through its partnerships and performances in New York, the Alvin Ailey American Dance Theater continually reinforces the importance of cultural exchange and understanding within its own community.

Alvin Ailey's "Revelations" serves as an inspiration for dance companies across the globe, encouraging them to embrace diversity, seek meaningful collaborations, and use their art as a tool for social justice. With each performance, workshop, and collaboration, the Alvin Ailey American Dance Theater cement their legacy as a driving force behind community engagement and cultural exchange in the dance world.

Influence of different cultural traditions on Ailey's choreography and artistic vision

" As a pioneer in modern dance, Ailey's artistic journey was deeply influenced by diverse cultural movements and techniques, resulting in a unique blend of African American and global inspirations. Throughout his career, Ailey actively engaged with communities and embraced cultural exchanges, incorporating elements from various traditions into his choreography.

Ailey's understanding and incorporation of African American movement and technique was pivotal in shaping his artistic vision. His exploration of African diaspora and folklore culminated in his magnum opus, "Revelations. " This iconic piece, which captures the spirit, struggles, and joys of African American history, showcases Ailey's commitment to preserving the cultural heritage through dance. By drawing upon the traditions of blues, spirituals, and gospel music, as well as the physicality and symbolism of African rituals, "Revelations" became a powerful representation of the African American experience.

Beyond the African American cultural realm, Ailey was also an avid traveler, continuously seeking inspiration from different parts of the world to enrich his artistic language. His interactions with diverse cultures profoundly impacted his choreographic style. For example, during a trip to Brazil, Ailey encountered capoeira, a Brazilian martial art that combines dance and acrobatics. Fascinated by its fluidity and grace, Ailey incorporated elements of capoeira into his choreography, creating a fusion of styles that added a dynamic touch to his performances.

Another cultural tradition that greatly influenced Ailey's work was his exposure to the dance techniques and traditions of other countries. Throughout his career, Ailey collaborated with international artists and dance companies, creating a space for cross-cultural exchange. These collaborations allowed him to explore movement vocabularies and choreographic approaches from different parts of the world, expanding his repertoire and pushing the boundaries of dance. By embracing cultural diversity, Ailey's choreography became a testament to the power of unity and inclusivity.

Moreover, Ailey's commitment to social justice and education was intricately connected to his engagement with communities and his drive to champion equality through the performing arts. The Alvin Ailey American Dance Theater, founded by Ailey, became a hub for nurturing talent from all walks of life. Through its community engagement initiatives, the company brought dance into underserved communities, offering dance education to children and adults, and leading transformative workshops. Ailey's understanding of the connection between dance and social justice permeated his choreography, enabling him to tell stories of resilience, hope, and empowerment.

The legacy of Alvin Ailey continues to inspire generations of dancers and choreographers, as his ability to seamlessly incorporate different cultural traditions into his work remains profoundly influential. By fusing African American movement and technique, global inspirations, and a commitment to social justice, Ailey created a unique artistic vision that reflected the vibrant tapestry of cultural diversity in New York and beyond. His ability to bridge divides and build bridges through dance elucidates the power of movement as a catalyst for change and unity within communities and across cultures. As we continue to explore the rich tapestry of dance and cultural exchange, Alvin Ailey's legacy serves as a guiding light, reminding us of the transformative potential of art and the importance of honoring different cultural traditions.

Chapter 11: Theatrical Productions and Collaborations

Ailey's collaborations with other artists, musicians, and designers in creating theatrical productions

Over the course of his career, Alvin Ailey forged numerous collaborations with artists, musicians, and designers to bring his theatrical productions to life. These collaborations were an integral part of his artistic process, allowing him to create groundbreaking works of dance that revolutionized the world of African American modern dance.

One of the key aspects of Ailey's collaborations was his ability to fuse dance with live music. He understood that the combination of movement and music created a more powerful and emotive experience for his audience. In many of his works, he worked closely with musicians to create original scores that complemented and enhanced his choreography. For example, in his seminal piece, "Revelations," Ailey drew on traditional African American spirituals as the basis for the music. He collaborated with composers like James Miller and Howard A. Roberts to arrange these spirituals, adding another layer of depth and cultural significance to the piece.

In addition to musicians, Ailey also collaborated with designers to create visually stunning productions. He understood the impact that sets, costumes, and lighting could have on the overall storytelling of a piece. For example, in his production of "Blues Suite," Ailey worked with set designer Carmen de Lavallade to create a realistic and evocative representation of a 1930s nightclub. Through their collaboration, they were able to transport the audience to a specific time and place, enhancing the narrative of the dance.

One of the most notable collaborations in Ailey's career was his partnership with the Alvin Ailey American Dance Theater. Founded in 1958, the company provided a platform for Ailey to showcase his choreography and collaborate with a talented group of dancers. Together, they brought his vision to life, performing his works on stages around the world. The company became a hub for African American dancers, providing them with opportunities and paving the way for future generations. Ailey's collaboration with the Alvin Ailey American Dance Theater not only created extraordinary performances but also left a lasting legacy as a pioneer of African American dance.

Ailey's collaborations were not limited to the world of dance and music. He also collaborated with educational institutions and community organizations to bring dance to communities that may not have had access to it otherwise. He believed in the power of dance as a tool for social change and used his collaborations to promote education and diversity. For example,

Ailey worked with the New York City Public School system to create programs that integrated dance into the curriculum, providing students with both artistic and physical education.

These collaborations allowed him to fuse different art forms and cultural influences, resulting in groundbreaking works of African American modern dance. From his collaboration with musicians to create original scores, to his partnership with the Alvin Ailey American Dance Theater, Ailey's collaborations were instrumental in shaping his legacy as a pioneer of the art form. Moreover, his collaborations extended beyond the stage, using dance as a means to promote social justice and education. Through his collaborations, Ailey not only inspired and expressed himself artistically, but also created a sense of community and made a lasting impact on the world of dance.

Exploration of diverse themes and styles in his choreography for the stage

Alvin Ailey, a pioneer in African-American modern dance, is renowned for his contributions to the world of dance, particularly through his groundbreaking choreography.

One of the key keywords that emerges from this exploration is "movement." Ailey's choreography is characterized by its dynamic and expressive movement, which reflects his deep understanding of African American cultural heritage. Through his intricate and energetic dance sequences, Ailey sought to convey the rich tapestry of African American history and experiences.

Another central keyword is "technique." Ailey was known for his mastery of various dance techniques and his ability to seamlessly blend them together. His choreography incorporated elements of traditional African dance, ballet, jazz, and modern dance, giving his works a unique and versatile style. The application of diverse techniques allowed Ailey to express different emotions and narratives, ensuring that his choreography resonated with a wide range of audiences.

Ailey's commitment to social justice is yet another vital aspect of his choreographic exploration. It is clear that he used dance as a platform to promote equality and challenge societal norms. Through his powerful storytelling and use of movement, Ailey addressed issues such as race, discrimination, and social inequalities. His choreography became a catalyst for discussions on these important matters, sparking dialogue and opening hearts and minds to the struggles faced by African Americans in society.

Furthermore, Ailey's focus on education plays a crucial role in the thematic diversity of his choreography. He understood the transformative power of dance and its potential to educate and inspire communities. Ailey established his own dance company, the Alvin Ailey American Dance Theater, which became a space for both professional dancers and aspiring ones to be nurtured and trained. Through his educational initiatives and workshops, Ailey not only set out to create exceptional dancers but also to cultivate a deep appreciation for African American culture and history.

Additionally, Ailey's collaborations with other artists and organizations expand the spectrum of themes and styles in his choreography. His collaborations spanned across different disciplines, including theater, music, and visual arts. By working with artists from various backgrounds, Ailey effectively merged different artistic languages, resulting in the creation of multidimensional and captivating works. These collaborations allowed Ailey's choreography to transcend the boundaries of traditional dance and engage with broader artistic expressions.

The legacy of Alvin Ailey and his exploration of diverse themes and styles in choreography continues to resonate today. His artistry, creativity, and commitment to social justice serve as an enduring inspiration for dancers, choreographers, and audiences alike. The Alvin

Ailey American Dance Theater, with its continued performances worldwide, keeps his vision alive, showcasing the power of movement and the transformative impact of dance on communities.

Through his masterful blending of movement techniques, his commitment to education and community, and his collaborations with other artists, Ailey created a rich and varied body of work that remains influential and relevant in the world of dance. His legacy as a pioneer in African American dance continues to inspire and ignite passion in the hearts of dancers and audiences around the globe.

Impact of staging and visual design on the overall experience of Ailey's performances

Chapter II specifically explores the impact of staging and visual design on the overall experience of Ailey's performances. This chapter sheds light on the significance of staging and visual elements, such as set designs, lighting, costuming, and props, in accentuating the power and essence of Ailey's choreography and the cultural importance it represented.

Dance is a multifaceted art form, and Ailey revolutionized the world of modern dance by infusing it with African-American cultural experiences and narratives. Through his impactful works, such as "Revelations," Ailey presented the struggles and triumphs of the African-American community, often highlighting themes of social justice, education, and community engagement.

Staging, as a crucial component of any theatrical performance, played a pivotal role in complementing Ailey's vision and bringing his choreography to life. Each performance space became a stage for expression and exploration, allowing Ailey's movement technique to be seen and felt by the audience. By carefully crafting the spatial dynamics through staging, Ailey's performances transcended mere physical movements and embraced emotional and spiritual dimensions.

The Alvin Ailey American Dance Theater, headquartered in New York City, became the stage upon which Ailey's artistic vision was realized. The theater's physical design and technical capabilities were instrumental in enhancing the overall experience of Ailey's performances. The use of state-of-the-art lighting equipment and design elements allowed for the creation of atmospheres that enhanced the mood and dynamics of the choreography. Whether it be a dimly lit stage to evoke intimacy or a grand display of lighting effects to highlight the liveliness of a dance, these visual elements engaged the audience on a sensory level and deepened their connection to the performances.

Moreover, the production designs for Ailey's performances were integral in shaping the cultural significance and impact of his choreography. Costuming played a crucial role in establishing the context of the dance and visually representing the cultural heritage of the African-American community. The choice of fabrics, colors, and styles were carefully curated to evoke emotions and enhance the storytelling aspect of the choreography. By utilizing traditional African garments, as seen in "Revelations," Ailey paid homage to his roots and conveyed powerful narratives of struggles faced by African-Americans throughout history.

In addition to costuming, props were thoughtfully employed to support the storytelling and movement motifs within Ailey's performances. The use of props, such as umbrellas, sticks, or chairs, added depth and layers to the choreography and further enriched the visual experience for the audience. These visual elements served as extensions of the dancers, amplifying the messages being conveyed through their movements.

Ailey's performances, underpinned by thoughtful staging and visual design, left a lasting impact on both the artistic and social realms. His innovation in the use of space and visual elements broke new ground in contemporary dance, inspiring future choreographers and performers to think beyond the confines of movement alone. By interweaving African-American history, social justice themes, and a deep sense of community, Ailey's performances embodied a powerful form of artistic expression that resonated with audiences from all backgrounds.

Through his pioneering works, Ailey merged dance, choreography, and African-American cultural heritage, creating a rich and transformative theatrical experience. The staging, lighting, costuming, and props were all instrumental in enhancing the emotional connection between the audience and the profound narratives Ailey sought to tell. These elements enabled the movement to transcend dance and transformed Ailey's performances into immersive and thought-provoking art forms. Ailey's legacy lives on, inspiring dancers, artists, and audiences to embrace the transformative power of dance and collective expression.

Chapter 12: Revisiting New York: Ailey's Homecoming

Ailey's connection to the cultural landscape of New York City

Alvin Ailey's connection to the cultural landscape of New York City is a significant aspect of his legacy as a pioneer of African-American dance and social justice.

At the heart of Ailey's connection to the cultural landscape of New York City is his dance and choreography. As a modern dancer, Ailey revolutionized the art form by infusing it with the rich heritage of African-American movements and traditions. His most acclaimed work, "Revelations," is a prime example of this fusion, as it draws inspiration from African-American spirituals, gospel music, and the blues. Ailey's unique movement style and technique resonated deeply with audiences, sparking a cultural movement that profoundly impacted the dance world.

The cultural significance of Ailey's connection to New York City is further emphasized by the social justice implications embedded in his work. Ailey's commitment to addressing socio-political issues through dance was revolutionary. His performances not only entertained, but also provided a platform for marginalized communities to express their stories and struggles. By blending artistry and activism, Ailey challenged societal norms and encouraged dialogue about race, identity, and inequality. His work became a catalyst for change, inspiring generations of artists to use their talents as a means of social commentary and progress.

Education was another important aspect of Ailey's connection to the cultural landscape of

New York City. Recognizing the power of dance as a transformative tool, he established the Alvin Ailey American Dance Theater and its associated school, providing opportunities for aspiring dancers to receive professional training. By offering scholarships and community outreach programs, Ailey made dance accessible to individuals who may have otherwise been excluded. This commitment to education fostered a sense of community and helped to break down barriers between different socio-economic backgrounds, contributing to the cultural diversity of the city.

Ailey's performances in the theaters of New York City further solidified his connection to its cultural landscape. From his early days performing at venues such as the 92nd Street Y to taking the prestigious stage of the Lincoln Center, Ailey captivated audiences with his artistry and talent. These performances not only showcased the brilliance of his choreography, but also generated a sense of pride and ownership over the cultural contributions of African-Americans in New York City. Ailey's presence and impact in these iconic theaters are an integral part of the city's artistic fabric.

Furthermore, Ailey's connection to the cultural landscape of New York City extended beyond performance spaces. His presence in the community, both through outreach programs and collaborations with local artists, solidified his influence and legacy. Ailey's inspiration and expression of his African-American heritage resonated with New York City's diverse population, fostering a sense of unity and celebration of cultural identity.

Through his dance, choreography, and commitment to social justice, Ailey fundamentally changed the landscape of modern dance and how it is perceived. His legacy as a pioneer and advocate for African-American artistic expression continues to inspire and empower artists in New York City and beyond.

Relationship with other arts organizations and venues in New York

Alvin Ailey was undeniably one of the most influential figures in the world of dance, particularly within the realms of modern dance and African American culture. His innovative choreography and dedication to social justice have left an indelible mark on the dance community, both in New York City and globally. In his autobiography, "Revelations of African-American Dance and Social Justice," Ailey delves into the profound impact that his relationship with other arts organizations and venues in New York had on his career.

One of the primary relationships emphasized in Ailey's book is his connection with the Alvin Ailey American Dance Theater. Ailey founded this renowned dance company in 1958, viewing it as a vessel to express his unique blend of modern dance and African American heritage. The company became a home for talented dancers who shared his vision, and together they expanded the boundaries of dance as an art form.

Throughout the book, Ailey highlights the crucial role that other arts organizations and venues played in supporting and promoting the Alvin Ailey American Dance Theater's groundbreaking work. The company frequently collaborated with prominent New York theaters such as the City Center and Lincoln Center, allowing their performances to reach wider and more diverse audiences. By forging strong relationships with these venues, Ailey was able to showcase his choreography and spread his message of social justice to a larger platform.

Additionally, Ailey acknowledges the significant influence that other artists and organizations had on his creative process. He frequently sought inspiration from various art forms, including music, literature, and visual arts, which informed his choreography and shaped the distinctive cultural movement that he pioneered. Ailey's collaborations with composers such as Duke Ellington and John Coltrane brought an exciting fusion of dance and music to the stage, further emphasizing the intertwinement of different art forms.

In terms of social justice, Ailey looked beyond traditional dance stages to address injustices in the wider community. His desire to create meaningful change prompted collaborations with organizations like the NAACP and the United Negro College Fund. Ailey's dance works often carried powerful messages of resistance, resilience, and hope, aiming to evoke empathy and provoke dialogue on important social issues. By establishing relationships with these advocacy groups, Ailey utilized dance as a medium to push for societal change and challenge the status quo.

Education was another central aspect of Ailey's legacy, and he understood the power of nurturing young talent within the dance community. The book underscores his commitment to providing opportunities for aspiring dancers and choreographers, particularly from marginalized backgrounds. The Alvin Ailey American Dance Theater's educational initiatives, such as the Ailey School and the Ailey/Fordham BFA Program, exemplify

Ailey's dedication to fostering the next generation of artists and expanding access to quality dance education.

Lastly, Ailey frequently emphasizes the unique nature of the dance community in New York City. The city's vibrant artistic landscape, filled with renowned theaters, dance companies, and diverse audiences, served as a catalyst for Ailey's creative endeavors. New York's energetic and culturally rich environment allowed Ailey to find his voice as a choreographer and gain recognition on a global scale. Without the support and collaboration of various arts organizations and venues in New York, Ailey's impact on the dance world may not have reached the heights it did.

His collaborations and partnerships with theaters, advocacy groups, and fellow artists were instrumental in shaping his legacy as a pioneer in African American dance and social justice. By leveraging these relationships, Ailey was able to showcase his revolutionary choreography, promote social change, and inspire generations of dancers. His story serves as a testament to the transformative power of dance and its ability to forge connections between diverse communities.

Impact of the city's diversity and energy on his artistic inspiration

Alvin Ailey, a renowned African American choreographer and dancer, found the city of New York to be a rich source of diversity and energy that greatly influenced his artistic inspiration.

Through his mastery of modern dance and the creation of his seminal masterpiece "Revelations," Ailey demonstrated the power of movement in depicting the African American experience. His choreography was deeply rooted in his cultural heritage, and New York City provided the perfect backdrop for his artistic expedition. The city's spirit of diversity allowed Ailey to constantly engage with various cultures and traditions, enabling him to develop a unique movement vocabulary that resonated with audiences worldwide.

The cultural diversity of New York City not only inspired Ailey, but it also served as the foundation for his exploration of social justice themes in his work. As an African American pioneer in the world of dance, Ailey approached his art with a strong sense of inclusivity and the desire to shed light on the struggles faced by his community. The city's dynamic atmosphere instilled in him a sense of urgency and determination to address social issues through movement.

Moreover, New York City's thriving artistic scene provided Ailey with countless opportunities for collaboration and artistic growth. The Alvin Ailey American Dance Theater, which he founded in 1958, became a hub for creative expression and community engagement. Ailey was able to cultivate a diverse pool of dancers who shared his vision and passion for dance as a means of cultural and social elevation. The theater became a platform for showcasing the profound impact that African American art could have on a global scale.

The energy of New York City acted as a constant catalyst for Ailey's creativity, fueling his desire to continuously push boundaries and redefine what was possible in dance. The city's dynamic rhythm and pulsating heartbeat became ingrained in his choreographic choices, breathing life into his performances. Ailey's artistic expression was not only shaped by the city's physical energy but also by the cultural and social dynamics that surrounded him. This amalgamation of influences allowed him to infuse his work with a sense of authenticity and relatability that touched audiences universally.

The city's cultural mosaic provided him with a wealth of artistic inspiration and allowed him to develop a movement technique that was uniquely African American. Furthermore, New York City's vibrant atmosphere and the city's commitment to social justice empowered Ailey to create masterful works that addressed important societal issues. Through the Alvin Ailey American Dance Theater, Ailey was able to further his artistic legacy and uplift his community. The city of New York will forever remain an integral part of Ailey's artistic journey and his relentless pursuit of dance as a vehicle for meaningful expression.

Chapter 13: Maintaining Ailey's Vision: The Future of African-American Dance

Challenges and opportunities facing African-American dancers and choreographers today

This chapter highlights the impact of African-American dance and explores the cultural, social justice, educational, and performance aspects of this art form. In this essay, I will discuss the key challenges and opportunities for African-American dancers and choreographers today, focusing on their engagement with modern dance, the importance of cultural movement and technique, and the role of African-American dance in social justice, education, and community.

Modern dance has provided both challenges and opportunities for African-American dancers and choreographers, as it serves as a platform for innovation and expression. Since its inception, modern dance has been largely influenced by white creators and performers, which has often marginalized African-American dancers. However, in recent years, there has been a growing recognition of African-American contributions to the development of modern dance. This acknowledgement has opened doors for dancers and choreographers to reclaim their narrative and showcase their artistry on a wider scale. A prime example of such recognition is the establishment of the Alvin Ailey American Dance Theater, which has played a pivotal role in promoting African-American talent and enabling them to make their mark in the field of modern dance.

Cultural movement and technique play a significant role in African-American dance, presenting both challenges and opportunities for dancers and choreographers. African-American dance encompasses a rich tapestry of cultural influences, including African, Caribbean, and African-American traditions. This diversity amplifies the challenges African-American dancers face in preserving their heritage while also adapting to contemporary dance styles and techniques. Moreover, these dancers must confront stereotypes and stigma surrounding their movement choices. However, embracing their cultural background also presents opportunities for African-American dancers to infuse their performances with a unique, authentic quality that resonates with audiences worldwide. By celebrating their cultural heritage, African-American dancers contribute to a more inclusive and diverse dance landscape.

Furthermore, African-American dance has long been intertwined with social justice movements, serving as a powerful tool for advocacy and empowerment. African-American dancers and choreographers have used their art form to shed light on issues such as racial inequality, discrimination, and social transformation. They have created performances that challenge societal norms and push boundaries, fostering dialogue and introspection. This engagement with social justice issues allows African-American dancers and choreographers to create work that not only captivates audiences but also inspires and educates people from all walks of life. By using their platform as artists to advocate for change, these dancers contribute to a more equitable society.

Education is another vital aspect of African-American dance that poses challenges and presents opportunities for dancers and choreographers. Access to quality education and training is crucial for the growth and development of aspiring African-American dancers. Unfortunately, systemic barriers can hinder their access to dance education, limiting their opportunities to hone their skills and pursue a career in the field. However, there are organizations and initiatives working towards bridging this gap and providing equitable opportunities for African-American dancers. By addressing these educational challenges, dancers and choreographers can nurture new talent and cultivate the next generation of African-American dance innovators.

Lastly, African-American dancers and choreographers have the opportunity to build and contribute to a vibrant and interconnected dance community. The legacy of pioneers like Alvin Ailey continues to inspire and guide African-American dancers. The Alvin Ailey American Dance Theater, located in New York, stands as a testament to the power of African-American dance in fostering a strong sense of community and artistic collaboration. By nurturing this sense of community, dancers and choreographers can support and uplift one another, creating an environment that embraces diversity, artistic exploration, and collective growth. This collective effort fosters unity and enables African-American dancers and choreographers to overcome challenges collectively, creating a supportive network for future triumphs.

From grappling with the nuances of modern dance, preserving cultural movement and technique, engaging in social justice initiatives, and ensuring equitable access to education, the journey for these artists is laden with obstacles. Nonetheless, through perseverance, innovation, and community building, African-American dancers and choreographers have the opportunity to showcase their unique artistry, challenge societal norms, and uplift their communities. Their work serves as a testament to the power of dance as a transformative agent for cultural expression, social justice, and personal empowerment.

Importance of preserving Ailey's legacy and artistic vision for future generations

Preserving Alvin Ailey's legacy and artistic vision is of utmost importance for future generations. Ailey's contributions to dance, specifically African American modern dance, have been monumental both artistically and culturally. Through his work, he not only revolutionized the dance world but also brought attention and recognition to the African American experience. His groundbreaking choreography, most notably exemplified in his signature piece "Revelations," has not only stood the test of time but also continues to inspire and move audiences.

Ailey's legacy is more than just his extraordinary talent as a choreographer and dancer. He was a pioneer in promoting racial representation and equality within the field of dance. At a time when African Americans, especially dancers, faced exclusion and discrimination, Ailey provided a platform for them to excel and showcase their talent. By forming the Alvin Ailey American Dance Theater, he created a space that celebrated African American culture, movement, and technique and provided opportunities for African American dancers to shine. This commitment to inclusivity and diversity laid the foundation for the future of African American dance.

Preserving Ailey's artistic vision is not only about ensuring that his works are performed and celebrated but also about carrying forward the underlying messages he conveyed through his choreography. Ailey's works often touched upon social justice issues and shed light on the African American experience, creating a platform for empathy and understanding. By exploring themes of community, oppression, and spirituality, Ailey's choreography fostered a deep connection between the dancers and the audience. It sparked conversations and challenged societal norms, encouraging viewers to reflect on their own attitudes and actions. Preserving Ailey's artistic vision means preserving these powerful messages and ensuring they continue to resonate with future generations.

Education plays a crucial role in preserving Ailey's legacy and artistic vision. By sharing his works with young dancers and students, we ensure that they are exposed to Ailey's unique style and perspective. Through education, we pass down the techniques and movements that make Ailey's choreography so distinctive. Moreover, we introduce young minds to the cultural significance behind his works, allowing them to appreciate the rich history and depth of African American modern dance. By incorporating Ailey's choreography into dance curricula and workshops, we inspire future generations to explore and expand upon his legacy, keeping his artistic vision alive.

Performances are another essential aspect of preserving Ailey's legacy. By staging his works in theaters across the globe, we expose new audiences to Ailey's artistry and provide opportunities for dancers to interpret and embody his choreography. These performances serve as a testament to the impact Ailey has had on the dance world and ensure that his works are not forgotten. They allow viewers to witness firsthand the beauty, power, and emotional depth of Ailey's creations. By continuing to perform his works, we honor Ailey's legacy and ensure his artistic vision is accessible to all.

The Alvin Ailey American Dance Theater, based in New York, plays a pivotal role in preserving Ailey's legacy and artistic vision. As the custodian of his works, they have the responsibility to maintain the authenticity and integrity of his choreography. Through their performances and outreach programs, they not only celebrate Ailey's legacy but also train and groom talented young dancers, empowering them to carry forward his artistic vision. As the torchbearers of his legacy, they have the opportunity to inspire future generations of dancers and ensure the ongoing preservation of Ailey's unique style and contributions to African American dance.

Ailey's groundbreaking contributions to dance, his commitment to racial representation and equality, and his powerful choreography have left an indelible mark on the dance world. By recognizing and celebrating his achievements, by continuing to perform his works, by educating young dancers about his unique style and cultural significance, and by supporting institutions like the Alvin Ailey American Dance Theater, we ensure that Ailey's artistic vision continues to inspire, challenge, and move audiences for years to come.

Strategies for promoting diversity, equity, and inclusion in the dance community

The chapter delves into the significance of Alvin Ailey's legacy in driving these initiatives, and it highlights key aspects such as dance education, performances, and overall community development.

Dance, as an art form, has always possessed the remarkable capability to transcend cultural boundaries and serve as a transformative medium for expression. However, for many years, the dance community has been disproportionately represented, with little recognition given to African Americans and their contributions. Ailey's pioneer work in modern dance challenged this norm and sparked the need for greater diversity, equity, and inclusion within the field. .

One of the key strategies for promoting diversity and inclusion is through dance education. By providing accessible and quality education to aspiring dancers from diverse backgrounds, the barriers to entry can be broken down. Offering scholarships, mentorship programs, and outreach initiatives can help build a more inclusive pipeline, where dancers from different racial and socio-economic backgrounds are given a fair chance to pursue their dreams in a supportive environment.

Moreover, the Alvin Ailey American Dance Theater, under the artistic and visionary leadership of Robert Battle, has continued to inspire and engage audiences worldwide. The theater's performances are a testament to the power of representation, showcasing the broad range of talent within the African American dance community. By addressing social justice and cultural themes in their choreography, the performances provide a platform to challenge existing narratives and facilitate meaningful dialogue around race, identity, and inclusivity.

Equally important is the cultivation of a supportive and inclusive community within the dance world. Creating spaces where diverse perspectives are valued, and where collaboration and dialogue are encouraged can foster an environment of respect and acceptance. Dance companies can actively seek out opportunities to collaborate and connect with artists from different backgrounds, creating a rich tapestry of cultural exchange and collective growth.

The legacy of Alvin Ailey serves as a powerful reminder of the transformative potential of dance. At the heart of his vision was the belief that dance is not simply a physical act, but a mechanism for social change. Ailey's commitment to telling the stories of African Americans through movement continues to inspire generations of dancers and artists to challenge existing norms and promote equity and inclusion.

By investing in accessible education and providing opportunities for dancers from diverse backgrounds, the barriers to entry can be broken down. Additionally, performances that address social justice and cultural themes create space for dialogue and representation. Creating an inclusive community that values diversity and fosters collaboration is equally essential. Ultimately, by following these strategies, the dance community can honor the legacy of Alvin Ailey and continue to push boundaries, inspire, and advocate for social change through the power of movement.

Conclusion

Reflecting on the enduring significance of Alvin Ailey's contributions to African-American dance and social justice

Reflecting on the enduring significance of Alvin Ailey's contributions to African-American dance and social justice, one cannot underestimate the profound impact he had on the cultural landscape of American dance. Alvin Ailey is renowned for his pioneering work in the field of modern dance, particularly for his iconic piece, "Revelations." This essay aims to explore the rich legacy of Alvin Ailey and the crucial role he played in promoting African-

American culture, elevating social justice issues, and inspiring countless artists and communities.

Alvin Ailey's journey began in a racially segregated America, where opportunities for African-American dancers were scarce. Despite the challenges and systemic inequality, Ailey navigated through adversity to shape the future of African-American dance. His choreography challenged existing norms by blending elements of traditional African dance, modern dance techniques, and gospel music. Through his innovative approach, Ailey redefined the boundaries of dance, captivating audiences with his compelling storytelling and profound emotional expression.

One of the key themes in Ailey's work was the exploration of African-American culture. In "Revelations," he weaved together the cultural heritage of his community, drawing inspiration from the experiences of African-Americans during slavery, the civil rights movement, and the ongoing struggle for equality. This piece showcases the resilience, courage, and hope of African-Americans, preserving their history and celebrating their spirit. Ailey's commitment to cultural preservation resonated deeply within the African-American community, empowering individuals and fostering a sense of belonging.

Beyond showcasing African-American culture, Ailey used his platform to address social justice issues through his art. He believed that dance had the power to challenge societal norms, provoke conversations, and inspire change. Ailey's performances often tackled themes such as racial injustice, discrimination, and the human experience. By shedding light on these pressing issues, Ailey not only provided a voice for the marginalized but also opened up dialogues about social justice within the predominantly white spheres of the dance world.

Ailey's dedication to social justice extended beyond his choreographic works. He recognized the need for greater access and representation in the dance world, particularly for African-Americans. In 1958, Ailey founded the Alvin Ailey American Dance Theater, creating a platform for African-American dancers to excel and thrive. The company became a glimmer of hope for aspiring dancers who had previously been marginalized, enabling them to share their talent, tell their stories, and inspire others. Ailey's commitment to education was also evident in his establishment of the Ailey School and scholarships for aspiring young dancers from diverse backgrounds.

Alvin Ailey's contributions to African-American dance and social justice have left an indelible mark on the world of performing arts. His legacy continues to inspire generations of dancers, challenging them to push boundaries, explore their cultural identities, and generate social change. Ailey's influence extends far beyond the stage, as his enduring significance lies in his ability to bring communities together, foster unity, and ignite conversations about race, equality, and justice.

His pioneering spirit, commitment to cultural preservation, and dedication to addressing social issues through his choreography have solidified his position as a titan in the world of dance. Ailey's bravery, resilience, and artistic vision continue to reverberate through the Alvin Ailey American Dance Theater and countless artists worldwide, ensuring that his legacy remains alive, relevant, and as impactful as ever.

Call to action for continuing his mission of cultural exchange, education, and artistic excellence

As a pioneer in the field of modern dance, Ailey revolutionized the world of dance by infusing it with elements of African-American culture, bringing forth a unique and powerful form of expression.

To continue Ailey's mission, it is vital to emphasize the importance of dance as a means of cultural exchange. Through dance, we can break down barriers, promote understanding, and celebrate the rich diversity of our world. By encouraging collaborations between artists of different backgrounds and cultures, we can foster a greater appreciation for our shared humanity and create a platform for dialogue and understanding.

Education also plays a crucial role in continuing Ailey's mission. Ailey believed in the power of dance education to transform lives and empower individuals. By providing accessible and high-quality dance education to communities around the world, we can give individuals the tools to express themselves, build self-confidence, and develop crucial life skills. Education can also serve as a means of preserving and passing down the rich cultural heritage that dance represents.

Furthermore, artistic excellence should be a guiding principle in continuing Ailey's mission. Ailey's choreography and performances were marked by technical precision, a deep understanding of movement, and a strong sense of artistic integrity. By upholding these standards and striving for excellence in our own artistic endeavors, we not only pay tribute to Ailey's legacy but also push the boundaries of what is possible in the world of dance.

Social justice is another essential element of Ailey's mission that must be carried forward. Ailey believed in the power of dance to uplift and bring attention to social issues. By using dance as a form of activism, we can shine a spotlight on injustices and advocate for change. Whether through thought-provoking performances or community engagement initiatives, dance has the potential to inspire and mobilize individuals to take action and work towards a more just and equitable society.

To continue his mission of cultural exchange, education, and artistic excellence, it is crucial that we value dance as a powerful medium of expression, prioritize education as a means of empowerment, strive for artistic excellence, and use dance as a platform for social justice. Only by embracing Ailey's principles and working towards these goals can we ensure that his legacy lives on and continues to inspire generations to come.

Acknowledgment of Ailey's lasting impact on the world of dance and his legacy as a pioneer and visionary

Alvin Ailey, the renowned American dancer and choreographer, has left an indelible mark on the world of dance. His contributions to the field, particularly in the realm of African-American dance, have been transformative. In his groundbreaking work, "Revelations: Alvin Ailey's African-American Dance and Social Justice," i explores Ailey's lasting impact on the world of dance and his enduring legacy as a pioneer and visionary. This essay presents an extensive analysis of Ailey's influence on the dance world and the significance of his work in shaping the cultural landscape.

Ailey's most prominent contribution to the field of dance is his establishment of the Alvin Ailey American Dance Theater. This theater, dedicated to showcasing African-American dancers and choreographers, provides a platform for their artistic expression and representation. Through the theater, Ailey aimed to break down racial barriers and challenge societal norms, showcasing the immense talent and potential within the African-American community. His vision of an inclusive and diverse dance company has continued to influence dance companies worldwide, pushing for the inclusion and recognition of underrepresented artists.

One cannot discuss Ailey's legacy without mentioning his seminal work, "Revelations. " This iconic piece captures the essence of African-American culture and portrays the struggles, spirituality, and resilience that define the experience of the African-American community. With its raw emotion, powerful movements, and evocative music, "Revelations" has become a timeless masterpiece in the world of dance. Its impact extends beyond the stage, serving as a catalyst for societal change and igniting conversations surrounding social justice.

Ailey's exploration and incorporation of African-American experiences through dance challenged the euro-centric norms prevalent in the dance world at the time. He embraced the cultural heritage and traditions of African-Americans, infusing them into his choreography. This fusion of African and African-American movements, sometimes referred to as the "Ailey technique," introduced a fresh perspective to the world of dance. By blending traditional African movements with modern dance techniques, Ailey created a distinct style that celebrated African-American culture while challenging the conventional notions of what dance could be.

In addition to his artistic contributions, Ailey's dedication to education and community outreach remain integral to his legacy. He believed in the transformative power of dance for individuals, particularly those from marginalized communities. Ailey recognized that dance had the ability to inspire and heal, providing an avenue for self-expression and empowerment. Through various educational initiatives and outreach programs, he extended the reach of his dance company and brought the joy of dance to countless individuals who may not have had access otherwise. Ailey's commitment to accessible dance education has laid the groundwork for the democratization of dance, enabling individuals from all walks of life to discover their passion and potential.

Alvin Ailey's impact on the dance world continues to reverberate to this day. His pioneering efforts have paved the way for African-American dancers and choreographers, ensuring their rightful place on the world stage. Furthermore, Ailey's dedication to social justice through his art has expanded the discourse surrounding race, identity, and equality. Through expressive movement, Ailey was able to provoke powerful emotions and challenge societal norms. His legacy serves as a testament to the transformative power of art, demonstrating that dance can transcend barriers and ignite meaningful change within society.

His contributions, both as a pioneer and visionary, have shaped the cultural landscape of modern dance. The establishment of the Alvin Ailey American Dance Theater, the creation of "Revelations," the fusion of African and African-American movement techniques, and his commitment to dance education highlight Ailey's enduring legacy. His work continues to inspire new generations of dancers and serves as a reminder that dance can be a vessel for expression, social justice, and community building. Through his dedication and passion, Alvin Ailey has left an indelible mark on the world of dance and has forever changed its future.

Printed in Great Britain
by Amazon